At the Harbourside

About the author

Rev Anthony Buckley works for the Church of England. He has taught history in Hereford, been a vicar in Folkestone and is now a school chaplain in London. Over the last twenty five years he has had countless conversations about faith and is in frequent demand as a speaker and writer. This book was written for those interested in Christianity, but who did not want to be pushed...

He is married with two children, a dog, a cat and one of the finest collections of Elvis CDs this side of Memphis...

At the Harbourside

Anthony Buckley

Highland
hb

First published by AuthorHouse in 2010. This revised
edition published in 2012 by Highland Books. 2 High Pines,
Knoll Road, Godalming, GU7 2EP

Scripture quotations taken from the HOLY BIBLE, NEW
INTERNATIONAL VERSION

The quotation from Martin Luther King on page 70 is taken
from Stephen B. Oates *Let the Trumpet Sound,* p.105,
Harper & Row, 1982.

ISBN-13: 978 1897913 88 8

ISBN-10: 1-897913-88-5

Printed in the United Kingdom by CPI Cox & Wyman Ltd,
Reading.

Contents

Sincere thanks to the many people who helped with the development of this book: fellow travellers from Alleyn's school, Southwark Diocese, Canterbury Diocese, Houseparty (Urban Saints) at Bethany School, and St. Barnabas, Dulwich. Their wisdom, criticism and guidance have been invaluable. And to Philip Ralli of Highland Books for all his patience and insight. He was probably right that my scribbled picture on a paper napkin did not make the final cut... And to Monica, Frances and Richard, who have spent rather too many evenings hearing the tapping of computer keys.

Chapter 1

At the harbourside

Imagine...

You are standing by a harbour and you are wondering whether to take a journey.

Or, more accurately, you know you are already on a journey but are wondering about the next stage. You wonder if you have been invited to consider a particular boat, bobbing in the water below you. There are steps to go down, the gangplank is lowered and you are free to walk across. You know a little about the boat and the crew but would like to know more. You are aware that you will not be captain and you are not quite sure where the wind will blow.

Whatever brings you to the harbour side, you are here.

It may have been a steady, deliberate, journey to this point. Or a new opportunity or relationship has arisen and we have found ourselves asking the 'Who am I'/ 'Where am I going' questions. Perhaps there has been an event of deep personal significance that has stopped us in our tracks. Perhaps we have heard stories about this boat and wondered if it was worth a closer look. It may simply be a sense of being tired and needing to rest. Or perhaps we don't really know why we are pausing at all.

Our busy lives may mean that these resting-places are difficult to find and we do not often stop to consider the journey we are on, or wonder where we are heading. We may not even want to ask these questions, and so this harbour side, attractive to others, is uncomfortable to us.

Gazing at the various boats in the harbour, we realise that they do not all offer the same journey or destination. In accepting an invitation to board any of them we are saying something about our own desires and longing, as well as the seaworthiness of the boat itself.

We may have had a good journey so far, and want to take many of those memories with us. Or our path to this point may have been difficult and we wish to leave much of it behind. Either way, we probably want to know that our journey, and

our experiences in it, have some sort of significance.

And what might we be searching for? It is one
of the most significant questions we can ask. It
is likely that our thoughts on this will depend at
least partly on our journey so far. We will have
been shaped by our experiences, relationships,
supposed or real successes and failures. We may
have been affected by advertising and media images; we may desire something because someone
else thinks we should have it, even though deep
down it is not what we ourselves long for. Or,
quite simply, we may not know what we are looking for.

This short book is an attempt to consider some
of the questions we face as we wonder about con-
tinuing the journey on board the Christian 'boat'.
It is hoped that it is of some value both to those
who are already part of the crew and equally to
those wondering about getting on board for the
first time. What is the boat all about? Will I be
welcome? What is life like on board? Will my
journey, my hopes and dreams, be appropriately
valued – neither ignored nor wrongly indulged?
Will there be things to learn? Is the boat really
there or is it all just a trick of the light on the
waves?

The harbour side is a good place to be re-minded that there is a journey to be continued. Time passes, things never stay exactly the same and we never stay exactly as we are.

If the boat imagery works for you, enjoy it. If it does not, ignore it. It is the content, not the wrapping, that matters.

To consider

* Why have you picked up this book?
* "We probably want to know that our journey, and our experiences in it, have some sort of significance." – Do you agree?
* How do you feel about your journey so far to this point? How has it shaped you?

Chapter 2

What holds this boat together?

A boy once sat next to me in a meeting. The speaker asked the audience: "What do you want for Christmas?" People called back with all sorts of answers, mostly electronic and well advertised. The boy looked at his shoes and said simply: "Love." His family was going through a difficult time; he knew that this was the one thing that truly counted, more than any gadget that might be on offer. The defining characteristic in Christianity is this same word, the word that speaks most deeply to our needs. This is the word that holds the boat together.

The core belief of Christianity is this: God loves us. He enjoys our company and wants a relationship with us. He constantly seeks to renew and restore this relationship. The love of God is not one-way, we are to be caught up in it: responding, sharing and receiving. Christianity asserts that our deepest desires are to do with being loved and being able to love. Whatever the weather and scenery on the journey, whatever the experiences we face, our innermost needs are to do with love, to do with being valued.

In John's account of the life of Jesus, recorded in the Bible, we are told that God so *loved* the world that Jesus was given. The night before he died, Jesus reminded his disciples that their love was to be the defining feature of their lives. Before that, he had told them that all the great commandments can be summed up in love for God, neighbour and self. In case the early church forgot this, its leaders kept emphasising the importance of love when they wrote to new believers.

In some ways it would be easier if the key characteristic was something else. Targets such as religious observances, leading a good life, not doing too much harm (or, at least, not being caught too often), are attractive and straightforward. We could work down the list; we could tick the boxes. Love is much more complex. It means that the journey is going to be personal and it will be about relationships: God-wards and neighbourwards. Our vulnerabilities may be exposed; we may have to face up to what we really are.

But of course love is liberating as well as challenging. Here lies depth and growth, and here is something anyone can receive and anyone can give. You do not have to be bright or strong, rich or articulate, to love. A child can love as richly as a king. We sometimes sense that we cannot truly live our lives richly by ticking boxes of various achievements and experiences. Christianity confirms this sense: it says that life is much more organic, more relational and more human, because love is at the core.

But what is love? It is not the same as indulgence; a parent who allows a child to eat whatever they want whenever they want is not acting out of love. It is not the same as a constant flow of warm feelings; a friend will visit a needy person because it is the right thing to do, whatever the feelings might be. It is not the same as paternalism; love is to be received as well as given. Perhaps it could be said that "Love is relentlessly wanting the best for the person", whether that person is ourselves, someone else, or God himself. What is the core value of this boat? What is the key belief at the heart of it? It is the belief that God loves us and wants the best for us. Utterly.

This belief stems from the idea that God not only loves, but he himself is love. For the early church, the first Christian group that gathered after Jesus' time on earth, there was a particular issue that had to be thought through. They had grown up in the Jewish faith and believed that there was only one God. But here was Jesus who had been God-like in much of what he said and did. Then Jesus talked about God's Holy Spirit being among them in a different way again. This was becoming very difficult to grasp. Were there three Gods after all, one God expressed in three ways, or would some other description fit?

They came to believe that the one God was 'Trinity', a relationship of three: Father, Son and Holy Spirit. They remembered that Jesus had told his followers to baptise new members of the Christian family in the name, not names, of the Father, Son and Holy Spirit.

It is difficult enough trying to articulate what really happens within the relationships in a family, even more so when describing the three-in-oneness of God. It would have been much simpler if the church had not articulated this belief; the fact they did says something profound about their courage to accept all the evidence as they saw it, even though it was so difficult to fit into a neat, labelled pack. And, of course, if God is real, with all the unimaginable depth and splendour that his existence implies, then it is unlikely we can easily understand his nature. There will be mystery and deeper truth than we can grasp.

In spite of the difficulty of fully comprehending or explaining this, the early church taught that in the very being of God there is community and fellowship. The love of the Father, the love of the Son, the love of the Spirit. One God, Trinity, constantly seeking to share love with us, including the child sitting next to me at the Christmas meeting.

To consider

- What might it mean to be truly loved?
- "Love is relentlessly wanting the best for the person" – Do you agree?

Chapter 3

Who is the captain?

Who is the captain? Who is going to see us safely through? Christianity is a religion focused on a person (hence the name). If we set off from the harbour side we are not led by a cleverly drawn map or a tidal chart, a guidebook or a handbook of self-sufficient sailing techniques; we are to be led by Jesus Christ. (Jesus was his birth-name; Christ was the title given to him.)

To talk about Christianity without focusing on Jesus Christ is like playing football with no ball. We may run around, we may wear the outfit, we may know our positions and practise our moves. It may be a good spectacle, but without the ball it is worth nothing.

An early church leader, Paul, wrote in his letter to the Colossians that Jesus is the expression of the invisible God. He is our role model and our guide. We look to him; in doing so we are looking to God.

If we are to start with Jesus, where to begin? Whatever one's faith position is, it is clear that something extraordinary happened in a small part of the Roman Empire in what we now call the early 30s AD. This was to shake and transform that empire and then affect the whole world. It was never claimed to be about a revolution, a scientific discovery, a book or a war; it was all about a person.

The claims made for Jesus have not been made for anyone else in history. If they are to be explored, then our minds may need to recalibrate to be open-minded enough to see all the evidence. There will be a little more on this in a later section when we explore some of the evidence for faith; for the present we will note what his contemporaries and near-contemporaries recorded.

They noted that he emphasised the inward qualities as much as the outward ones. He commented scathingly on those who wanted status for its own sake and who loved being the centre of attention. He said direct and uncomfortable things about materialism and about giving to the poor. He stressed accountability and integrity.

We are told that Jesus spoke with particular authority. He gives the impression that 'this is how it is, whether you like it or not' and sees himself as playing a central role: he is the author who has walked on to the stage and he knows the direction that the play is taking. It is he who will ultimately call people to account, returning to wrap this world up when the time is right. It is he who can lead us to full relationship with God and to rich, deep eternal life – life in all its fullness.

The most shocking part of his teaching and actions was that they pointed to him in some manner being God. He could forgive sins, the deliberate wrongdoings we do to others and ourselves and thus to God; this is an enormous claim: not only sins committed against him, but *anyone's* sins. He had the power of the creator over illness and death, he was able to still the stormy waters, to feed five thousand people and turn water into wine. He saw himself as being outside linear time. He claimed to offer spiritual nourishment that will last forever; he could see people safely through death into a new life beyond the grave.

The reaction was as you would expect: hardly anyone quite fully believed it, some people were deeply offended, and some were scared. And some wondered: could this be the one…?

He was kind to people who were isolated, mocked, and not in the mainstream. He spoke words of comfort, truth and welcome to the marginalised, to tax collectors, traitors, the sick, children, women, the thief on the cross, even a centurion in the occupying Roman army. He was happy to talk openly in the market place or to receive nervous inquirers quietly and privately.

There are moments of courage and action (No, you are not going to stone that woman // Yes, I am turning over these tables which you use to cheat people who come to worship // Yes, I will mix with those you call undesirables – and you'd better look out for your own eternal destiny rather than pretending to worry about theirs). It must have been exhilarating and dynamic being with him. People loved him, hated him, feared him, worshipped him, wondered about him – but no one ever said he was boring…

If he had been, they would not have bothered to crucify him. Some of the leaders of the province were worried that the watchful Romans would punish a new mass-movement. Perhaps also they were unsure of their status, and the status of the cherished magnificent temple, if all these marginalised outsiders were seen as welcome and you could be forgiven as easily (and more completely) by this preacher in a distant village as you might by performing complex rituals in Jerusalem. They knew that his claim to be God was blasphemous. Occasionally people say that Jesus did not claim to be God. Those who question this then need to ask why the religious leaders at the time seemed to have no doubt that this was exactly what he was claiming.

To be fair, not all the leaders were against him: Joseph of Arimathea, Nicodemus and some influential women, such as Joanna, were persuaded. The Roman governor Pilate was equivocal and was hesitant to condemn.

But enough were opposed to Jesus to build momentum for him to be crucified, executed as a common criminal. There was nothing glamorous or special about the way he died. It was a favoured form of punishment because it was public, humiliating, incredibly painful and 100% successful.

He had given earlier hints that his death was going to be necessary to provide reconciliation and healing between God and sinful humanity. Now it was happening, and the rest of the Bible is full of people discussing, quite excitedly, the significance of this death on the cross. They would look back and remember Old Testament prophecies such as the one recorded in Isaiah, chapter 53, "He was pierced for our transgressions, he was crushed for our iniquities; the punishment that brought us peace was upon him, and by his wounds we are healed."

But on that Friday their thoughts were probably far away from such weighty matters. Then all must have been dark disappointment and hopes dashed. The subsequent joyful reflections came about because of the extraordinary events two days later. Sunday morning, the tomb was empty and Jesus was talking to people. A new chapter, a new beginning. He was physical but also somehow more than physical. He ate fish but appeared in locked rooms. The marks of the crucifixion were still there, but he was not battered and broken. He was sometimes easily recognisable and sometimes not. It was not that he had come back *from* the dead, it was as if he had come *through* death. He was himself, but there was a difference.

It is not surprising they took time to believe it (they knew very well that dead men don't rise), but they could not get round the evidence in front of their eyes. The reaction was summed up in formerly-sceptical Thomas' acknowledgement: "My Lord and my God".

If there really is life after death, as hinted and glimpsed in faiths and emotions throughout human history, then our perspective on priorities in this life will need to change. If Jesus was God then the resurrection, this coming through death, was inevitable because death cannot hold God. If Jesus is stronger than death, then he really can forgive sins and offer eternal life. Whatever victory was won on the cross, it truly was won. Death need not hold us, either. If the resurrection happened then all his extraordinary teachings, claims and actions take on a new integrity and force. It is unsurprising that, in this boat, the focus is on the captain.

Does he ever get cross?

Jesus did not shout at the occupying Romans or the prostitutes, but he did get angry with hypocrites. As noted earlier, he criticised those who indulged in a deliberate misplacing of priorities, focusing on praiseworthy outward actions instead of the deeper issues of love and attitude.

Do we deliberately give an impression on the outside that does not match what we are thinking on the inside? Note the word 'deliberate'. Of course we do things from mixed motives and we want to appear at our best. It becomes a problem when we consistently, deliberately, choose for the outside to be different to the inside. It is dangerous when we wear a different mask so that we burden others, either by condemning them for sins which we are perfectly happy to allow to fester in the hidden places of our own hearts, or by pretending to be what we are not, hoping they will feel inadequate in comparison.

When Jesus said that we were to be like children one characteristic he was perhaps affirming, alongside the virtues of love, trust and humility, was transparency. You know where you are with a toddler; what you see is what you get. As we grow up we become very skilful at separating the inside and the outside. The inconsistencies that this creates can be very harmful to ourselves and to our relationships. Much of Jesus' teaching was about sorting out what goes on in the inner person, knowing that this then shapes the outside. Too often we are tempted to worry only about appearances. We do well to remember his question: "What good is it for you to gain the whole world, yet lose or forfeit your very self?"

We should note that, as well as showing frustration with hypocrites, Jesus made it crystal clear that those who sought to harm children were heading for deep trouble. There is a cold and certain anger in his words on this issue. The cries of the vulnerable, whether children or others, will not go unnoticed.

He also got angry with those who put up barriers for others to express their faith in God. Thus the tables at the entrance of the temple were turned over.

The captain is full of love and compassion, but that does not mean that anything goes. Quite the opposite, it is *because* he is full of love and compassion that true justice will be exercised.

To consider

- What would it have been like to be with Jesus?
- What did you think of this brief description of Jesus?
- Should some points have been emphasised more and some less?
- Why is hypocrisy so destructive to real relationships?

- How good is our society at looking after the vulnerable?

Chapter 4

Where does prayer fit in?

Some readers may feel this is all getting a bit religious! Perhaps you feel you are only gazing from a distance at this boat but you have already been asked to ponder love, the Trinity and Jesus, and this chapter heading looks distinctly 'religious'. But then another part of you wants to know what you might be taking on – and prayer is so much at the heart of Christianity that it needs to be looked at early on.

Christianity is not primarily about doing certain things or upholding a set of values, although these are deeply important. It is first and foremost about relationship and thus the concept of prayer is important for the serious enquirer. Prayer holds the crew and captain together in one team. Without it we do not stay in touch with the captain.

The word 'prayer' may make us uneasy...

Perhaps we think it is a religious thing to do and we are not sure we are religious.

Perhaps we don't think it works.

Perhaps we don't know where to start.

We do not have to be a certain type of person, be in a church building or use particular words, to pray. Heading into a crisis, many people ask something or someone 'out there' for help. In the middle of a wonderful experience, many people want to express thanks to something or someone bigger than the immediate. When regretting a wrong action or word, many people want to say sorry in the deepest places of the heart and hope there is a possibility of forgiveness. Prayer is as natural and as important as a child speaking to an adult who cares.

Thought-provoking, and even a little daunting, is the Christian belief that prayer is seriously important and used by God to change things. It may not be in the same way that we were expecting, but often it is, which is very exciting and humbling. Our prayers, however they are answered and however feeble they might feel to us, are profoundly significant.

But what about when prayers seem to be answered 'no'? We follow in significant footsteps when we feel this happens. Before he was arrested Jesus asked if there was not some other way of carrying out his mission, but it was not to be. He had already entrusted himself to the will of God and did not fight against this answer. Prayer is not filling a supermarket trolley – "I'll have some of that today, Lord"– prayer is a committing to relationship with God wherever it might lead, sharing our requests, fears or thanksgivings. It is about trusting we will be resourced for the journey even, perhaps especially, when it is not the path we want or choose. If we sometimes think prayer does not work, perhaps it is because we are expecting it to do the wrong thing. It is not a slot machine; it is the expression of a relationship.

Where to start? Some people use prayers that others have written, some use a pattern such as 'T.S.P.', standing for 'Thanks, Sorry, Please'. Some people listen to music, go for walks, write or draw as they pray. Some simply speak or think what is on their heart. Many value praying with others. Some enjoy being still, quietening the words, internal and external, and learning to listen. Giving space to hearing the quiet voice of God.

Any words will do, but it is helpful to have a structure and Jesus himself has given us a golden pattern in what, with a small addition at the end, is now known as 'The Lord's Prayer'.

* * *

The Lord's Prayer

Throughout the Bible and church history there are thousands of prayers recorded for our encouragement; all that are truly valuable pick up an emphasis that can be seen in the Lord's Prayer. The more familiar version is used here:

Our Father, who art in heaven,
hallowed be thy name;
thy kingdom come;
thy will be done,
in earth as it is in heaven.
Give us this day our daily bread.
And forgive us our trespasses,
as we forgive them that trespass against us.
And lead us not into temptation;
but deliver us from evil. Amen.

Here is a brief interpretation:

We note that the first word is 'Our', not 'My'. Whenever we pray we are united with the vast host of people around the world and through history who pray to God. We never pray alone even if physically we appear to do so. We are not sailing a boat on our own. The second word reminds us of the perfect paternal love of God (for those who have difficult memories or images of fatherhood, we can think in terms of "a thousand times better than the best parent we can imagine") but that he exists outside of our limited world. This is no tribal god of a wood or a sea; this is the one God who is in heaven.

We are reminded that we are praying to a holy God, different from the created world. His name is hallowed; his love and purposes are pure and just. Perhaps implied is the thought that God can be honoured through our daily business, through right actions and attitude. In the same way that a head teacher is honoured by good behaviour of pupils, so God's name is honoured through our lifestyle.

We pray for the kingdom, the acceptance of God's authority, to continue to grow; we pray for evil and confusion to be pushed back step by step from apparent positions of strength. We look for, and are excited by, green shoots of love and faith, wherever we see them. The kingdom grows as our obedience grows. As part of this, may God's will be done in our lives.

It is daily bread we need, not a monthly stock of caviar: enough resources – emotional, spiritual, physical and intellectual – to face the challenges and opportunities of today. We are never promised a pain-free voyage. There will be storms and rocky places, but we can ask for enough to see us through the journey we are called to travel today. Tomorrow there will be other worries and different weather. The landscape may change. We will need to pray similar words again.

We are to be forgiven and forgiving people. If we do not think we need forgiving, we put ourselves outside the healer's reach. If we do not want to forgive others we are closing our minds to the forgiveness we ourselves need, and showing that we value the relationship and the person less than we value the sin or the grudge.

There is much discussion as to what Jesus actually meant by "Lead us not into temptation" (or "to the time of trial"). To take one slightly simplistic approach, it is wise for an alcoholic to pray that the off-licence will be shut, for the besotted man to pray that that girl won't be at the party. It is wise to pray that the difficulties we face will not throw us off course. There will be dangers on the way, not always immediately recognisable for what they truly are; we need to pray to be kept safe as we travel through them.

We finish the prayer by acknowledging that the power and glory is God's, not ours. He can see us safely through; it is his strength that counts.

* * *

God wants us to pray; the relationship matters. If there are moments when we do not feel like it, moments when we realise we have not prayed for days or years and feel guilty or nervous about knocking on that door again, moments when we pretend we are too busy, then it is good to bring to mind that God wants us to pray. Remember, this all about love. He likes our company.

To consider

- Do you agree that discussing prayer needs to be part of an exploration of Christianity?
- Was this too early to do it?

At the Harbourside

- What helps us to pray?
- What hinders us from praying?
- What else could be said about The Lord's Prayer?

Chapter 5

Will I be welcome on board?

The welcome to the group should feel like coming home. The captain wants us to feel secure, he wants us to know we are safe, however unclear the journey may seem and whatever the weather. Coming home has long been an image of spiritual life, summed up in St. Augustine's prayer "Our hearts are restless until they find their home in you". In one of Jesus' stories the metaphor for the errant offspring's renewing journey is coming home.

But, as it is a true home, it is a place where business will be done. It is a place of growth and maturing. Guidance will be offered and behaviour sometimes challenged. There may be times when we will say: "Do I really want to change? I have got used to my habits and foibles, I know I am not perfect but I have made things comfortable for me and I know how things are." God, the best parent and the best teacher, has more ambitious plans for us than we do. We are not simply on a journey, we are being changed as we travel.

You are very, very welcome to join the group. The ethos of the boat is always meant to be welcoming to new members. It is not an exclusive club and if ever it appears to be, then it is forgetting its core value. Those who organise activities within the group always need to be mindful not to be introspective, nor to be full of jargon or assumptions.

Repentance

Part of accepting the welcome is being honest about ourselves. We may feel that we are clutching baggage that is going to be out of place on the boat. We may be very hesitant, conscious that we are carrying cheap plastic bags full of rubbish about to split at any moment, or heavy rucksacks, equally filled with rubbish, that are tightly bound to our backs. We may keep all this hidden by careful choice of clothes but we know it slows us down and entangles us with unnecessary distractions. And we are terrified of being found out.

The bags may contain tendencies to think that we are always right or that we always should be in charge; tendencies to want money or status above all else, to abuse sexual desire, or to hurt someone else simply because we have the power to do so. They may contain a secret inclination that shames us. Whatever may be in the bags, we will need to face up to it. We will need to say to the captain: "I want to journey with you but as I learn to be part of the group please help me get rid of these things which keep distracting and slowing me down." Our underlying attitude needs to be a desire to be rid of the things that spoil our relationships, wellbeing and potential. This is what Christians call 'repentance', a change of heart about our treasured sins.

Jesus will always respond; he longs to restore us. We are immediately forgiven, but we may not be immediately fully transformed; he tends to change, teach and unburden us at the speed that works for us. As with any healing, it can feel like a strange mix of rough handling and gentle soothing.

Baptism

Since the time of Jesus, a sign of welcome to the Christian journey has been baptism, the immersing in, or pouring over of, water. We are physical people and it is unsurprising that we can be helped by physical acts, or that they can be used as vibrant visual aids, and more, to help us. Baptism is known as a 'sacrament', a physical act with a spiritual significance. Communion is another sacrament, which we will reach in due course. Some branches of the church specify other sacraments. Some see all physical acts as having the capacity to be sacramental.

The washing of baptism symbolises new beginnings and cleansing. It is the sign of welcome into the family of God. It is as if the first thing that happens to us when we join the boat is that we are given a bath: not only good in itself but helpful as a sign of ongoing washing, refreshing and growing that will take place on the journey. It is believed that while God is somehow especially at work when someone is baptised, the person themselves needs to live out their baptism, seeing themselves as a fully welcomed and participating member of the team.

* * *

The gangplank is lowered and ready. All new travellers are very welcome (Jesus became quite frustrated with those who did not want 'new people' to join in). Baptism marks the welcome; repentance shows that we are serious about wanting to receive this welcome, and all it might mean for us.

To consider

- What does 'Home' mean to you?
- What makes a community of people a welcoming one?
- Is 'repentance' an exciting or a disturbing concept?

Chapter 6

Is the food good?

We will need nourishing for the journey; we do not, we cannot, successfully travel in this boat in our own strength. We will be strengthened in many ways: through friends and circumstances, prayers and experiences, examples and wisdom. There are two specific ways that are especially worth bringing to mind at this point: Firstly, the ceremony known to many as Holy Communion and secondly, the Bible.

Bread and wine

On the night before he died Jesus changed the familiar Passover words, used by Jewish people (Jesus was Jewish) when taking a special meal that included bread and wine, remembering escape from slavery in Egypt many years before, and applied them to himself. In effect he said: "I am the great liberator from the slavery of sin and death, all previous liberation moments have fore-shadowed me." He said that the broken bread and wine outpoured expressed his sacrifice on the cross to be made the next day. That it was also a victory meal, pointing towards the feast and joy of restored relationship with God that death cannot end. We are to take the bread and wine in memory of Jesus and as a special part of the way that he feeds and strengthen us. In some way that we cannot possibly hope to understand, they express Jesus himself.

As we meet with others in the group we may find that they call this service of bread and wine by all sorts of different names – The Eucharist (from Greek, meaning thanksgiving), The Lord's Supper, The Lord's Table, The Mass (from Latin, meaning we are 'sent out' into the world), Holy Communion (together with God, together with others). As ever, the name does not matter. What does matter is the spirit with which we receive it.

The sacraments of baptism and communion are gifts for us to receive and are seen as very important in the Christian church. Not surprisingly, their importance has led people to think care-fully about them, sometimes disagreeing about them. Sadly and unnecessarily, some have then allowed these disagreements to harden into divisions. This is inappropriate. When children are given wonderful gifts the proper response is a humble and grateful acceptance. They are unlikely to understand how the gift truly 'works'. Brash or insecure friends may pretend that they are the ones who really know why the train can go round the track, but the train set can be enjoyed and valued by everyone, whether or not they fully understand the laws of electricity.

What is going on? Jesus especially present in the faith of his people as they receive bread and wine? A wonderful memorial? Jesus especially present in the bread and wine themselves? It is too deep and rich to be fully understood; we are simply invited to take and eat. Christians throughout history have told the Jesus story while taking bread and wine in obedience to Jesus' command to do so. Love given and nourishment offered.

To consider

- Bread and wine, shared and received. Such a simple act, such a powerful one. Why does it matter so much to so many people?

A book in your hands

A great deal of what has been said so far has referenced the Bible. What sort of book is it and what is it for?

It is not a long manuscript dictated by angels. It is a collection of books written by people, with all the complexities of human emotion on display, which Christians believe is particularly inspired by God. This collection does not tell the whole story of the universe, past, present and future. The scriptures, 'the writings', have a specific purpose; they are to tell the part of the salvation story that we need to know and to guide us into right behaviour.

When we read or listen to a Bible passage we can remember the pattern 'P.T.P.' We are to be:

- *Prayerful* – That God would say something through it to us.
- *Thoughtful* – What is going on in this passage? It is helpful to imagine what it would have felt to hear these words in their original context.
- *Purposeful* – What can I learn from this about God, myself or my relationships?

There are numerous patterns of readings, commentaries and notes to help us. When reading narrative, longer sections work well; in other parts simply a verse or two will be enough. It is the quality, not the quantity, of our reading, that matters.

A very inadequate overview of the Bible might include the following summary. The Old Testament reveals some key characteristics of God, especially that he is one, creative, holy, just and loving. God's dealings with the people of Israel show what is expected of a community living and growing together, of his passion for them and indeed for the whole world. Through the Old Testament there is a recurring theme that a saviour figure is going to appear; the story is as yet incomplete.

The New Testament tells the story of the arrival of this saviour figure, named Jesus; of what happened to him and what happened next to his followers, the early church. A recurring theme in the New Testament, and foreshadowed in the Old, is that this Jesus will one day return, bringing endings and new beginnings.

Where to start? If you are new to this, Mark's Gospel is a good opening. The first four books of the New Testament, Matthew, Mark, Luke and John, are known as 'Gospels' because they tell the story, in slightly different ways, of the 'Good

News' (translation of 'Gospel') of Jesus. Another possibility is to use the suggested list of readings at the end of this book, (and there are many such lists available elsewhere). A Study Bible is very helpful. It is like having a teacher alongside you as you read the passage. Reading with a friend or a group is also very stimulating.

Sometimes people ask: Is the Bible literally true? We need to be careful with questions like this. If we were to say "James loves Matilda to bits", the meaning is clear: affection is strong. The imagery is, well, imagery; Matilda is not lying in pieces round the house. The Bible is full of different kinds of literature: history, lectures, letters, stories, dreams, poetry, visions. Sometimes different kinds are mixed in the same book. When Jesus tells one of his parables we are jumping between history and story in the same chapter. Sometimes there is no explicit indication that this jump is being made, but we sense that this is happening. It is fascinating to read parts of the Bible and try to work out what sort of literature it is, but the important point is that Christians claim that it all contains inspired, authoritative, helpful truth. The leader of the group may choose to share his wisdom by telling a story, singing a song, writing a letter. "Is this poetry or

is this prose?" is a less important question than:
"What is God wanting to say to me through this
passage?" The means are less important than the
meaning.

We soberly note that over the centuries, and
indeed in our own times, men and women have
given their lives so that words from the Bible can
be read in people's own languages. Our translations were made at a price.

Christians believe that the *acted* word of sharing the bread and wine of communion and the
written word in the Bible both point to the *living*
word, Jesus. He wants to resource us for the journey.

To consider

- Does the idea of reading the Bible seem easy
  or difficult?
- If you are going to begin reading, where will
  you start?
- If you are already used to reading the Bible,
  how is it going?
- What kind of Bible translations might work
  best for you? Do you prefer up to date and in-
  formal or traditional and stately?

Is the food good?

- Why do you think the writers of much of the Bible (and Jesus himself in his teaching) thought that telling stories was so important?
- Why might it be as important to read the Bible aloud, or to listen to it being read, as to read it silently?

Chapter 7

I feel a bit rubbish...

If you think you are perfect, this is not the group for you. The great news is that those who have joined this group know they have not got everything sorted out. Jesus stressed that he could only really do business with those who knew they were in need, who did not get everything right and who knew that sometimes, to be honest, they were not as pleasant as they would like to be. Forgiveness is always on offer and members of this group know that they need it.

A summary of Jesus' message might be: "I know what you are like, I know what you have done, and I would love to have you with us. In fact I would do anything, have done everything, to welcome you here."

Sometimes, sadly, people think they are too sinful or broken to join. Sometimes, wrongly, they have, explicitly or implicitly, been given this message by others. This is seeing things exactly the wrong way round. We are needy people. That's why we are here. We do not have to be good enough to take part; in fact, we *cannot* be good enough to take part.

The captain and crew of the boat want to welcome us as we are. We have not been invited because we have paid a membership fee or because we understand how to sail. We have not been invited because we have the best boots or can tie the best knots. We have not been invited because we have any 'rights'. We have not been invited because we are connected to someone already on board or because we have tried to be good for days, months or years.

We are invited because we are ourselves. God enjoys our company so much that he wants to spend eternity with us. Likes and loves us so much that Jesus came, at indescribable cost, to restore the relationship.

Thus we don't throw our weight around on this outing; we have no weight to throw. We have not earned our place; we have been given it. It is magnificently exciting and thrilling. For those

42

of us who like being in control, it is also a little unsettling. It is all about *grace*; it is a gift freely given.

To consider

- How do we get the right balance between knowing we are not perfect and knowing we are profoundly valuable?
- Is it uncomfortable to know that this is 'a gift freely given', rather than something we earn?

But... it's about the way I look

A teenager pointed out to me that for some of us, we do not feel rubbish because of our behaviour, we feel rubbish because of the way we think we look. We are not talking here about physical problems resulting from a bad lifestyle that are expressed in our appearance; if that is the case then questions need to be asked – What help do I need? What choices do I need to make? Nor is this about severe abnormalities that may need medical attention. This is a different issue, perhaps caused by years of exposure to false media images or even because of thoughtless comments from people around us. We do not think we look lovely, and so we think we are unlovable.

Five suggestions that may help restore a true perspective:

1. Those who love us think we look great. Beauty really is in the eye of the beholder. They are glad to see us and that includes what we look like because that is how we are. They may help us tidy ourselves up a little if that is needed for courtesy in certain situations, but they do not want us to have a different face. If we think they would love us more if we looked different, then we are misunderstanding what it is to love and be loved.

2. We do well to question the motives and reference points behind the drive for a certain 'look'. Does someone deliberately, skilfully, want us to feel negative about our appearance so they can make money selling us something we would not otherwise want? Watch the advertisements or articles carefully, and see through them.

3. Ask the big questions. Is western society currently scared of the ageing process? Does it

    sometimes over-emphasise sexual attraction? If so, what is happening in our cultural thinking in these areas?

4. Remember that right at the heart of Christian belief is that God loves you profoundly, utterly, as you are. What really matters is what you do and what you think, not what you look like.

5. Become informed about what is happening in the world and be reminded of those situations where survival, not appearance, is the issue. This always helps with our priorities.

To consider

- When Oliver Cromwell was having his picture painted he told the artist: "I desire you would use all your skill to paint your picture truly like me, and not flatter me at all; but remark all these roughness, pimples, warts, and everything as you see me; otherwise I will never pay a farthing for it."

- A starving child is not interested in what you look like; he or she only wants to know if you are going to help.

- When we think of people who have changed the world or have personally inspired us, do we think of their personality or their appearance?

Chapter 8

...But I do want to play by the right rules

Back to behaviour: we often get it wrong, but something deep in us wants to get it right. Part of love is that we want to play by the right rules and to hear the right guidance so that we don't hurt others. If we are going to join, we want to be a help, not a hindrance. Part of accepting an invitation to a party is wanting to know how to behave when we get there.

The athlete was overjoyed. He had reached the finishing line first. Raising his arms in a celebration of victory he noticed that there seemed to be little applause. He looked around him and saw an official approach him. "The egg has to stay on the spoon," the man whispered.

Part of our deep desire to get it right may mean rethinking how we should be running the race. The athlete in the egg and spoon race had been using the wrong criteria. Our society bombards us with images about success and failure: get appearance, status or money right and you will finish the race in triumph. But what if these criteria are the wrong ones? We may think we are crossing the line to win but what if we were running the race according to the wrong rules? Some in the crowd may applaud, but perhaps they have got the rules wrong, too?

In the eyes of Christ, if today is to be a successful day, then we will be living it with love, compassion, honesty and justice. It is not so much what we do, it is how we do it. We may make a large sum of money or be told we look amazing, but if we are not doing this in love then we have deeply failed. Conversely, we may make all sorts of mistakes and sometimes look stupid, but if we have managed to try to show a little love and faith on the way, then it has been a gold medal day.

Some of us can put up with nearly anything except the feeling that we have made a wrong decision. Perhaps it did not make us as happy or as rich or as famous as we thought. Perhaps it was part of a grand strategy that now seems to be unravelling. Perhaps we always prided ourselves on our discernment and wisdom, and now our friends are shaking their heads and believe we have lost our way.

But we may not have done so. It seems that in the eyes of God the 'how' we decide is as important as the 'what'. If we choose to do something thoughtfully, prayerfully and lovingly, then it is the right decision. If we are manipulative or selfish in the decision-making, it is the wrong decision.

We will soon realise that the captain is as interested in our thoughts as in our behaviour. Members of the group are called to attend to their inner selves, not at the expense of outward actions, but rather so that these actions can be properly shaped and resourced. Paul urged his readers in the early church in Philippi to fill their minds with good things: "Whatever is true, whatever is noble, whatever is right, whatever is pure, whatever is lovely, whatever is admirable – if anything is excellent or praiseworthy – think about such things."

This list is well worth using as a reference point as to what we watch, read, listen to and think about. Perhaps newspaper editors, television producers and computer programmers should have it on the walls of their offices. If we are going to *do* good we need to *think* good.

Jesus said that the greatest commandments were to love God and love others as we love ourselves. He said that these summed up the commands given in the Old Testament. The most famous of these were the Ten Commandments. These words were given to the Jewish people as they were being formed into a community and a nation. In some present societies where there seems to be an uncertainty about the validity of any kind of rules at all, it is helpful to see the themes that underlie the words. Here is a slightly abbreviated version, with brief reflections. (We may see links to the Lord's Prayer and to what is called Jesus' 'Sermon on the Mount', recorded in Matthew 5-7.)

A community begins to be formed... Exodus 20:1-17

> I am the Lord your God, who brought you out of Egypt, out of the land of slavery. You shall have no other gods before me.

There is one God. There are not thousands of tribal deities inhabiting woods or hills, each one being equally valid and offering equally valid guidance. There is one God, listen to him. He is the God who is part of our story and he is the God who rescues.

> You shall not make for yourself an idol in the form of anything in heaven above or on the earth beneath or in the waters below. You shall not bow down to them or worship them.

We are not to worship an idol, putting all our resources into chasing man-made objects or man-imagined dreams. An idol will not deliver what we need and it distracts our attention from God.

> You shall not misuse the name of the Lord your God.

We are to see God's name honoured; 'name' is tied closely to identity in biblical thinking. We should be careful about our choice of words. (What is going on when people constantly say "Oh my God!"?). We should similarly be very careful about doing things in the name of God if we are using that phrase as a cover for our own motives and agenda, not his. It is all too easy to manipulate others through religion.

> Remember the Sabbath day by keeping it holy. Six days you shall labour and do all your work,

but the seventh day is a Sabbath to the Lord
your God. On it you shall not do any work,
neither you, nor your son or daughter, nor your
manservant or maidservant, nor your animals,
nor the alien within your gates.

We are to live a balanced life, especially ensuring
there is a balance between work and rest. We
note that the command to keep the Sabbath includes a command to help other people keep it.
Workaholics not only harm themselves; they are
also deeply unhelpful role models for others.

Honour your father and your mother, so that
you may live long in the land the Lord your God
is giving you.

We realise that society has a structure; security
and stability demand that we work within it. For
those with difficult or absent parents, we can
widen the applications to the parental figures in
our lives, but we should not ignore the implicit
emphasis on the family that these words carry.
We need to make the most of the wisdom and experience of the older generations; it is a win-win
result if they know that they are honoured and
valued.

At the Harbourside

You shall not murder.

We do not have the freedom to take someone's life just because we feel like it. It sounds obvious, but think of the difference to our streets and our homes if everyone obeyed this, and we knew that they obeyed it. There is also the implication that strength is always to be guided by morality. We are commanded to protect, not crush.

You shall not commit adultery.

I was once with a class of non-religious teenagers who, unprompted, wondered if adultery should be illegal. They had seen the damage it had done to their families. On reflection, they understood that the issues are often complex and it is not always easy for outsiders to see quickly the whole picture, but their feelings remained strong. Self-discipline, faithfulness, commitment and honesty are all caught up in this, as is the obvious issue of sexual self-control.

You shall not steal

We are not to steal people's possessions or anything they hold dear – their dignity, reputation, relationships or hopes.

> You shall not give false testimony against your neighbour.

We are not to lie about other people. Wherever we are, whatever the context or motive, we should not manipulate words to cast another person in a bad light.

> You shall not covet your neighbour's house... or anything that belongs to your neighbour.

It does not make us happy if we envy and desire someone else's possessions or reputations, and it destroys the relationship we have with them. It shows that we have forgotten that we are loved and valued as we are (as are they).

Obedience and trust

Sometimes the captain tells us to do something. We may not understand why and we may not feel like doing it, but a wise member of the crew will do it anyway. Jesus wants us to obey, not because he is power-hungry (he is not needy like that) but because he really does know what is best for us.

Thus, a helpful question for travellers is not really "Am I having a good experience?" or "What can I get out of this moment?" A better question is "How can I be obedient in this situation?"

How do we know what we are being asked to do? The guidance comes in many ways – through people, the church, Bible reading, praying, circumstances, our thinking – and it will always be consistent with the nature and purposes of God.

Underlying obedience is trust. The captain does not issue arbitrary commands for the sake of it; he is someone whom we can trust. Sometimes we will travel at a different speed than we expect. There will be unexpected pauses or obstacles, times when the journey is easier than expected and times when it is harder. There may be times when the way is especially foggy and we feel detached from him or our other companions. We need to hold in mind the core belief that we are precious and loved in his eyes.

What does 'trusting in God' look like? Beginnings of answers may include: feeling confident that he will lead us safely through, that the promises of forgiveness and renewal are secure. Believing that his guidance is indeed the best way to live, even though it may jar against some other attitudes in our society.

To consider

- What are the criteria for success and failure that we use in our lives?
- Where did we find them?
- What values would you like to be shown in your life?
- Do you think the Ten Commandments are still relevant today?
- Which ones do you need particularly to consider?
- If we are not trusting and obeying God, then what are we trusting and obeying?

Chapter 9

Too much information or not enough?

We are standing at the harbour side, comfortably leaning on the railings in the morning sun and looking at the boats. We might be wondering by now if we are getting too much information! Surely it is fine simply to join the boat and learn as we go?

And of course it is, many do that and that is right for them; we are all different and we are encouraged to maintain our individuality. At the other extreme there are some who want every detail covered and who are very hesitant about taking a single step; the thoughtfulness is commendable but they may need to be careful that this hesitation does not lead to avoidance; we cannot stay still for ever. Like any step of faith (getting married, moving house, choosing a career) there is a limit to what we can know until we begin the journey, and of course the learning does not stop then.

But for those who feel a little bombarded by what you have read so far, it may be useful to remember that Christianity is not complicated, but it is deep and it is rich. At its heart is this: God loves you and loves the world. You are invited to believe this and respond to it.

The depth and richness lie in the unpacking of the truths that these words express. They also lie in the self-evident fact that, if God exists at all, then there is going to be mystery and always more that we can explore. They lie in the truth that you and I are complex, intellectual and emotional beings. If we want a faith or way of life that is not deep and rich, that is easy to understand completely, then we are looking for something that is too small to be real and is unlikely to satisfy for very long.

It keeps us humble. A great deal of the trouble caused by religion is when people think "My group is the only group that *really* understands how God works." At that point they forget that God is bigger than them; they also close themselves to the possibility of learning more; they despise or fear others for not seeing things in the way that they do. To put it crudely, a central part of the revelation about God in the Bible is that this is a 'big' God. Not some tribal idol that we can call up when we want, nor an easily-understood reflection of the particular desires or prejudices of a small group. This is God himself: in the beautiful 55th chapter of Isaiah we are reminded that "As the heavens are higher than the earth, so are my ways higher than your ways and my thoughts than your thoughts."

Part of accepting that this is a 'big' God is accepting that our understanding will never quite be big enough. An exciting and important part of this is then accepting that presumably God can have an equally full and deep relationship with an inarticulate mentally handicapped person, or with a tiny baby, as he can with a professor. God is not going to be limited by our lack of intellectual understanding. If he were, then he would not be God.

It is difficult to measure the moment when we say 'This person is my friend.' It can be a growing process or it can be a sudden realisation. We may know a great deal about them or very little. But at some point the friendship seems worth pursuing and we hope that the more we discover the more the friendship will be strengthened.

Too much information or not enough?

This has faint echoes of a growing relationship with God. Different people may feel they need different levels of information before accepting the invitation; the important thing is to remember that the invitation still stands.

Chapter 10

What about my fellow travellers?

If we ponder getting on board the boat we may wish to know more about our fellow travellers. When we hear the word 'Church' many different things, positive and negative, may come to mind.

A speaker once sketched this imaginary scene:

When Jesus returned to heaven after his time on earth, the angels asked: "What happens now with your wonderful plan for renewing humanity and indeed the whole world, for ushering in a new kingdom of love and justice?"

Jesus replied that he was leaving things in the hands of a few followers in and around Jerusalem. One angel looked at the collection of confused and uncertain men and women, whose track record of understanding and courage was not, to be honest, all that great. He gulped and paused, and then nervously asked: "Excuse me, Lord, and what's plan B?"

"There's no plan B," Jesus replied.

And there wasn't, and there did not need to be. For those ordinary people were renewed by God's Holy Spirit. The church was born. One of the extraordinary features of history has been the growth of the Christian church from such inauspicious beginnings: a criminal's death on a cross, a near-unbelievable claim of life renewed, a motley collection of followers and here we are two thousand years later. The church has grown faster since 1900 than in any previous century. No need for plan B.

As he was preparing to complete his earthly ministry Jesus promised that God's Holy Spirit would guide and strengthen his followers. The Spirit is not physical; he is not limited to one place as Jesus was during his time on earth. Jesus could not be in Jerusalem at the same time as he was in Bethlehem. The Spirit can.

The Spirit is alongside and he gives gifts. The early church learned that these God-given gifts are offered for the benefit and encouragement of all. This is not like being on a cruise ship where, if you wish, you can go the whole journey locked in your own cabin and pretending the other passengers do not exist. This is a shared journey, encouraging each other, looking after each other. We are all in the crew. We are to play our part, and help our neighbours play their part. They will have skills and gifts that we do not have; we will have gifts that they do not have and we should not keep them hidden. There are several lists of gifts recorded in Paul's letters to the early church; some may seem exotic, some may seem ordinary. All are seen as valuable and vital to the wellbeing of the whole.

It is a gifted and a fruitful group. Paul was a key figure in guiding the early church as it tried, in various locations, to work out what it meant to be followers of Jesus. In his letter to the Christians in Galatia, chapter 5, he describes the 'fruit' of the Spirit as "love, joy, peace, patience, kindness, goodness, faithfulness, gentleness and self-control."

There is not space here to comment in detail on each of Paul's definitions but, for example, we may note that:

Gentleness is not easy if we are in a situation where people want obvious displays of power. But in reality true strength is seen in gentleness. Anyone, sadly, has the physical ability to hurt a baby; gentleness comes in using the strength to protect, not to crush. The same can be said of all our relationships; it is vital to learn to hold, not to squeeze.

Patience similarly is a sign of strength and trust. To have the courage to wait, to know that we do not need to force the issue, to know we do not have to get there first. The Spirit can set us free from the fear that causes us to insist on our 'rights' now.

In his first letter to the Corinthians, chapter 13, Paul describes what love looks like: "Love is patient, love is kind. It does not envy, it does not boast, it is not proud. It is not rude, it is not self-seeking, it is not easily angered, it keeps no record of wrongs. Love does not delight in evil but rejoices with the truth. It always protects, always trusts, always hopes, always perseveres. Love never fails."

Are any of these qualities particularly unfashionable or ignored in the company we keep? We may be in situations where faithfulness and self-control are mocked. There may be people, perhaps ourselves, who rather enjoy keeping records of wrongs. We may be in circles where self-seeking is held up as a virtue. The pressure on us not to fulfil the demands of love may be stronger than we think.

Tragically, the love that Paul proclaims, that defining characteristic of Christianity, does not always flow from what we call 'the church'. Sometimes immense pain and hurt has been done by 'church' people. Perhaps through ignorance; sometimes (it seems) through a bizarre desire to think about anything else except the example of Jesus. Perhaps because there is no genuine prayer, no keeping in touch with God. They may do terrible things to other people while not acknowledging that this is the last thing the captain would want them to do. They may forget that they are to love people.

Sometimes our fellow travellers will get things out of perspective. They may get obsessed with a particular issue and forget the big picture ("I will only sail with you if you have yellow shoelaces like me. In fact, all the yellow shoelace wearers will stick with me at the back of the boat; I will worry so much about yellow shoelaces that I will stop listening to the captain. And if I did listen to him, I would only want to know what he has to say about yellow shoelaces").

Individuals, and the human institution known as 'the church', have got many things wrong over the centuries. This is unsurprising, as it is filled with people like you and me who do not always make good decisions. There have been failures, inevitably, and some devastatingly sad and cruel acts. But it is a matter of historical record that individuals and the institutional church have also got a very large number of things right; think of schools, hospitals, soup runs and countless offers of comfort and care; think of the millions of people encouraged to serve neighbours and strangers day by day.

True church is about what we are and what we do. We *are* church; we do not *go to* church. Church is not a building and it is not an institution (When we call a building "a church", we are using shorthand for "in this building, the church meets". When we call a human organisation "The Church", we are using shorthand for "this is how some of these Christians choose to organise themselves"). There are good times when individuals and institutions manage to catch up with the real, spiritual church, spread magnificently and lovingly across all nations and through history. These are the times when people are playing their part, valued for what they are and what they can contribute, trying to be faithful in their praying, loving and obedience to God. But there are bad times when individuals or institutions do not express the love and wisdom of Jesus Christ. When that happens, it says more about them than it does about him.

(And of course it is an illogical jump to say that the misbehaviour of some Christians means that Christ does not exist. You could equally say that a football manager does not exist because one of his players fouled another.)

The early Christians met together, ate together, learnt together, prayed together. Underlying it all was a profound commitment to each other. Tradition has it that outsiders commented: "See how these Christians love each other". All ages, backgrounds, abilities were there. These are the fellow travellers: very human, often getting it wrong, but the ones whose hearts are in it are inspired by the captain to be gifted and fruitful. He does not wait for us to be perfect. The invitation, roles and tasks are prepared for us, as we are.

To consider

- What is most people's impression of 'church'?
- What do you think is God's vision for the church?

What about my fellow travellers?

- What might happen to our attitudes, relationships, our churches and our society if the 'fruit' of the Spirit were more evident?
- Two 'fruits' were briefly explored here; what would you say about the others?

Chapter 11

Will I just be lazing around?

A big challenge is to be ourselves and not pretend to be someone else. We are called by name: "Peter, Mary, come along and travel with us." We are called to accept that we are welcomed and valued as we are. There will be room to be ourselves and express our talents. There will be tasks to be carried out and work to be done. We are not sailing for the sake of it, nor for our own pleasure (although there will be a great deal of pleasure on the way). There are people to greet on our journey, neighbours to encourage, the needy to help, decks to clean, sandwiches to be made. We will encounter other boats and land on different islands; we are called to serve all whom we meet in whatever way is best.

In all parts of our lives we are entrusted with responsibility. Whether it is our homework, the report for the boss, the next course of bricks, the figures added up, the kneading of the bread, the saying of prayers, the visiting the lonely or the cleaning the oven, the work is to be respected. And those who work, we should honour.

We are using the word 'work' in its widest sense. There is no distinction in the Bible between the value of paid and unpaid work; it is all service to be done wholeheartedly in the name of God. There is no such thing as an unimportant task in his service.

We need to be careful that we are not tempted to think that the value of work is measured in terms of the size of the salary or the status attached to the role. We also should remember that those who manage others have a responsibility to honour the work of employees or volunteers and to ensure it is as interesting and fulfilling as possible. The mundane is valuable for what it achieves, not because it is mundane. It is thoughtless to keep tasks boring in themselves when, with a little thought and care, they could be developed and enhanced. How can a task be shaped and valued so that the person doing it can see satisfaction in the doing of it?

Martin Luther King said in December 1956: *"Whatever your life's work is, do it well.* A man should do his job so well that the living, the dead, and the unborn could do it no better. If it falls your lot to be a street sweeper, sweep streets like Michelangelo painted pictures, like Shakespeare wrote poetry, like Beethoven composed music; sweep streets so well that all the host of heaven and earth will have to pause and say, 'Here lived a great street sweeper who swept his job well'."

Whatever we are called to do on our journey, let's do it well. The hosts of heaven are watching. And doing things well might involve being appropriately focussed. If we are emailing while eating while watching TV while texting while chatting to someone in the room, then we may need to ask how well we are handling all the relationships involved. Busyness is not the same as quality.

Leadership

Most of us exercise leadership at some stage of our lives. It may be at work or at home; it may involve responsibility for a pet, a large and complex business, a tea trolley or a family.

On this boat the model of leadership centres on service. Jesus washed the feet of his friends the night before he died. The captain is not carried about on deck on a golden chair; he is cleaning the deck and hauling the ropes with us; he gets his hands dirty.

Selfish ambition will not be the driving force of our leadership. We will be willing to hear both sides and to see the whole picture before coming to a conclusion. We will be willing to build good relationships because this is the best way of knowing what is going on in the organisation and because there is a fundamental understanding that people matter.

There will be a focus on integrity. When we are leaders our behaviour needs to match the responsibility given. There will be honesty about our own mistakes and a willingness to help others through their mistakes. We are taking responsibility not because we are ruthlessly ambitious or we have fallen into it by accident; we are taking it because we have been asked by the leader to do it. We feel honoured to be entrusted with it. We may sometimes have to speak words of challenge or discipline to others; we will need to do so honestly but with concern for the person, whatever the shortcomings of the performance.

Part of understanding leadership is knowing when we are under someone else's authority. At certain times a chief executive is wise to obey a lollipop lady. I may be an expert at reading a map but I need your leadership if I am going to help make the sandwiches. The overall purpose will always be more important to good leaders than their personal status.

Witness

We are called to be honest. If we are part of this group, beginning to sense new reference points, new challenges and opportunities and a growing relationship with the leader, then it will be surprising if that remains unnoticed by others. Perhaps our attitudes and behaviour may be changing so our lifestyle may be speaking of new beginnings. And perhaps we will find that we are talking about faith as well as living it.

We are not to be formulaic. Jesus said different things to different people in different ways. He knew what they needed to hear and how they needed to hear it. Paul likewise spoke differently in different situations.

Someone told *us*. Almost certainly we are at the harbour side or already on the boat, at this point of consideration, because someone took the trouble to tell us or show us how the Jesus story fitted their story, and how it might fit ours.

We can be thankful for their commitment, and inspired by their example.

If we do not tell others, then who will?

To consider

- How do you honour work and responsibility?
- What good and bad leadership have you experienced?
- How do you feel about sharing faith?

Chapter 12

Well, I'd like to laze around a little…

A brief return to the fourth commandment. Our society can be quite a driven place. We may need to relearn the childlike ability to rest and to allow others to rest. We may need to learn that, in the eyes of this particular leader, the aspiration to achieve the right balance between relaxation and work, between the needs of family, friends and our employers, is more important than striving only for work-based targets. There will be times (on average, a seventh of our time but we are not to be legalistic about it) which should be given over for idling and ambling, enjoying what there is to be enjoyed. Reflecting on, and making the most of, our situation, our relationships and our faith.

Some may need to relearn the joys of harmless pleasures. Of course the adjective 'harmless' is vital; if we are harming ourselves or others then the activity will be destructive, not restful. We may have felt that fun and games should have long been put behind us, but there is a childlike and important humility in doing something simply because we enjoy it. A favourite book or walk, a time with friends. Hot chocolate and Beethoven. If we struggle to think, "What do I enjoy?" then it is too long since we did it.

Sometimes we say or do too much because we want to control a situation; we are scared of it slipping away and so we throw a net of words or actions all round it, closing off every escape route, pinning down anything that looks loose. On this journey we don't have to talk too much. We don't have to do too much, either.

Being quiet and restful means trusting that we don't have to nail everything down. It means we have time to hear the voice of the captain through others, circumstances, the church, our praying and our reading. Inner quietness is a mark of humility; it is a resting in the love and purposes of God.

It is not the same as opting out, of being detached from others or from situations. It is not the same as childishly thinking that we are above such things as laughing and chatting with friends. It is part of a Sabbath lifestyle, learning the liberating truth that we are only *part* of the team. We are not the captain, owner of the boat and entire crew rolled into one.

Being over-busy can even be a semi-deliberate ploy to shut off the voice of the leader and of others; perhaps this is why it is such an insistent theme in the Bible that we take time to be still, and to listen.

When the disciples rush to wake up Jesus during a storm on the Sea of Galilee, we read that he was resting his head on a cushion. We may think of heroes as stoical and pain-free, who think nothing of laying their head on a bare wooden deck. There may be times when this is appropriate, but we note that in this case Jesus used a cushion. Perhaps it was already on the boat, perhaps he had brought it with him, perhaps someone else brought it for him. Wherever the cushion came from, it was not spurned: a little bit of comfort was not seen as a bad thing.

Well, I'd like to laze around a little…

To consider

- How do you honour rest and leisure in your life?

Chapter 13

Sometimes, even though the sun is shining somewhere...

The weather may be good, the boat sailing well and fellow crew members smiling, but we may be inwardly troubled. What might these difficult times include? How might we face them?

Temptation (and mercy)

Sometimes we do wrong things; we let down others, the captain and ourselves. We will want to know the enemy, to be prepared for whatever may trip us up. Temptation is a personal area (what tempts me may have no hold on you, and vice versa) but there may be some general thoughts worth considering:

Underlying temptation to sin is the temptation to think that God has got it wrong, that he does not have our best interests at heart and that we know a much better way to achieve the satisfaction we crave. It is somewhat unlikely that we do.

Or perhaps we think that *this* time he will not notice.

Temptations promise so much but deliver so little. This is why some are addictive: we look for the next thrill because we hope, against all experience, that *this* time we will achieve what we are really looking for.

Another trick is to get us preoccupied with thinking we are winning a battle in a small area while the real attack is happening on undefended territory elsewhere. We think we are facing an attack on our determination to avoid eating three doughnuts each day, while in fact this is a feint; the real attack is coming in encouraging us to be increasingly selfish, spiteful or proud. We may not notice this more serious assault, or pretend we do not notice.

Being tempted is not sinful; the sin is falling to temptation. And sometimes we fall. We sense the chalice is poisoned but we still choose it. The crucial issue is what we do next. If we persist in holding it to our lips, drinking again and again of the poison, with no regret, then our wellbeing will suffer, deteriorate and eventually die. If we turn to Christ, honestly admitting that we have made the wrong choice in this particular action, thought or conversation, then he takes the cup from us and restores and nourishes us with forgiveness and love. Jesus' death on the cross is the focus for cleaning us up, for soaking up our sin. He took it all on him, experiencing the separation from God, from all that is good, that sin causes. In 1 Peter 2:24 we read, "He himself bore our sins in his body on the tree, so that we might die to sins and live for righteousness; by his wounds you have been healed."

The captain knows where we need to be going; he understands that sometimes, strangely, we scrabble out over the side of his ship to reach another craft that momentarily is glinting in the sun. If we turn our face back to the ship he will launch the lifeboats and welcome us back, bedraggled and covered in seaweed as we might be. Always.

Temptation can indeed be an issue for all of us; but when we think of it we should always equally consider forgiveness and mercy. In ourselves and with others we should be dismayed by sin, but never by the sinner. We can speak firmly against a bad act but we are never to crush the person.

We are to be gentle people, to ourselves and to others. If we can see that God longs to forgive us for what needs to be forgiven, and that this is a free gift, then inevitably we will want to be forgiving and merciful people. This is not the same as pretending that we do not sin or that no-one sin against us. It means facing up to the fact of the wrong done, acknowledging it and then saying that the relationship is bigger than the sin. We may be wounded enough that we need space from the person for a season, but we still value them and want the best for them.

Part of being merciful, and just plain sensible, is to realise that there is a difference between a mistake and a sin; they need to be responded to in different ways.

Part of living in mercy (receiving it and giving it) is being generous with our gifts, our time and our money. It is sad when we are mean-spirited rather than Holy-Spirited. Jesus said a great deal about not being trapped by the worship of money and similarly about the need to show charity to the poor. Our giving should be an expression of a free and giving nature, of a response to the divine generosity that we ourselves have received.

Feeling flat (and restoration)

Sometimes, unexpectedly, we can feel low. Fog obscures our way and all feels flat and grey. In 1 Kings 19 we read that the prophet Elijah had won a great victory against the prophets of Baal. The people of Israel had witnessed the power of God and the long-awaited rain had arrived. But instead of a warm glow of satisfaction of a job well done, Elijah felt very flat: "I have had enough, Lord".

Everyone else might be thinking that all is going wonderfully well and we do not have a care in the world, but inwardly we are saying: "I have had enough". Characters in the Bible are very honest about their tendency to get fed up. In the Elijah narrative we are given an example of what can be done to help.

Elijah was allowed to sleep and eat, sleep and eat. That was the beginning, as simple as that. His body was restored to normal rhythms.

He was then given a purpose. There is always something valuable that we can do. It need not be dramatic or noticed; there is great merit in doing the 'ordinary' things well. However we are feeling, God is active. We may not quite see what he is doing or how our small contribution fits into the bigger picture, but our lack of insight into these things does not stop him working through us.

He was then told he was not alone. Hard on the heels of feeling purposeless can be the feeling that we are isolated. Isolation through internal torment while everyone else appears to be smiling is very difficult. It is not always easy to articulate our feelings or even to know whether we should. It is good to remember that we are part of a big team, many of whom will have gone through similar experiences, and that it is very helpful to find the right person with whom we can share our sorrows. We do not sail alone, and we should not carry our burdens alone.

* * *

Sometimes we will know what has triggered the feeling of flatness. That may be a nudge to seek help and counsel. Events and situations matter; we are wise to be aware of their effects. Or we may not know the trigger but someone else, from a detached position, may be able to see our story more clearly.

We can be encouraged by the truth that when we feel flat we are not the first to have done so!

If we feel that this flatness may be symptomatic of medical depression, then it is entirely right to seek advice. There is a millennia-old Christian tradition (shared with other serious faiths) of affirming and encouraging medical expertise. It is a sign of strength, not weakness, to ask for help.

Doubting and questioning

We are whole people. Our minds like to be stretched and our feelings can fluctuate. This can be unsettling, even though it again follows the pattern of many people in Christian history. Later we will explore some of the evidence that can support faith, but with all the pointers in the world there will still be fog banks, when nothing seems clear or conclusive. Two brief thoughts at present:

First, if it is a question about our feelings changing then it is helpful to remember that God sometimes takes away feelings of peace and assurance because he does not want us to rely on the feelings in themselves. Comforting feelings are happy reminders, but the underlying Christian belief is that we are profoundly loved whether we feel it or not. We can see why these withdrawal moments are important; my feelings can be all over the place depending on weather, conversations or the performance of the England cricket team. If my faith is for real, it needs to be rather more foundational than that. When the feelings change, it may be less pleasant but it may not be a bad thing; it can help us to look to the core of what we believe and why we believe it.

Second, we will sometimes have specific questions. If our heart is to be exercised by loving then it is entirely appropriate for our minds to be exercised by questioning. If so, whom can we ask or what can we read to help with these? We are unlikely to be the first to ask such things and it is wise to see what others have to say.

There may be frustration. It is not easy to hold the balance between rigorous intellectual searching and the realisation that there will be some explanations beyond our grasp. If God is for real then some things will be beyond our understanding. As said earlier, the unsatisfactory alternative is a person-sized and thus person-invented religion.

Sometimes on the journey we will not understand what is going on, or why we are going in a particular direction. This is not the same as wondering if the leader truly exists, or that it is the wrong group. We may sometimes want to ask significant questions about the actions of our employers or teachers. We may not understand them or we may disagree with them, but we still believe that they exist.

Doubts and questions may be healthy but they can be disturbing, challenging and frustrating. This is not a sign that things are going wrong; indeed it can be a positive time if we end up being led into a deeper understanding.

To consider

- How do you face the temptations that particularly affect you?
- Do you find it easy to forgive and to be forgiven?
- Is it healthy to talk about doubts and questions?

Chapter 14

And sometimes the weather is just plain awful.

As well as internal pressures there will sometimes be difficult external factors; we will find ourselves in situations where we have to react to events outside of our control. These can sometimes bear down on us heavily as we feel exposed to the rain and the cold.

Taking an unpopular stance in an unjust world

We may be in a situation where others are being unjust. It is not enough to be kind, although that can be challenging; we are equally called to be stand up for justice and this may mean being unpopular. We should be putting right those things that are unfair. We are to protect the vulnerable; perhaps a colleague in business or someone in

our school who is always being put down or ignored, perhaps people further afield who can be
helped through legislation, campaigns or charity
work. The sea across which we travel is full of
situations and adventures that need our involve-
ment. That means that there will be times when
we challenge local powers or when we remind
them of their responsibilities. When we are called
to exercise authority ourselves, we have a particular calling to be models of justice.

As ever, we must start where we are. Part of
treating people fairly is learning to understand
our own motives. If I am determined to put person B in the shade so I am noticed by person C,
then I will manipulate situations and conversations to my advantage. Or, if there is an ongoing
feud with person D, I may read the worst into all
his words and not give him a fair chance. I am
not standing up for justice in either of these situations.

These dynamics happen in families and
churches as much as they do in workplaces and
schools. The question "Do I always treat others
justly?" would be a challenging exploration for
many of us. Even more so would be: "Do I stand
up for justice for others?"

And sometimes the weather is just plain awful.

We will not always get bouquets for taking such a stand.

Persecution

And there will be people who will laugh at us. In some parts of the world this mockery is hate-filled and leads to persecution and death. It is a sign of the insecurity of the mockers and the persecutors. If their philosophy or religion lacks the strength to cope with the ramblings of deluded Christians then they would be better occupied in checking the foundations of their own beliefs. But this truth does not make the pain and loneliness much easier to bear.

Jesus was crucified; many in the early church were martyred. Many still are. Even in those places where the scorn tends to be expressed in words, not in physical brutality, the cruelty can be real and effective. Jesus warned that this would happen: "Blessed are you when people insult you, persecute you and falsely say all kinds of evil against you because of me." Perhaps we can even say that the stones or insults being thrown at us as we walk are a sign that we are on the right path.

(But we should not go out of our way to encourage or provoke the stone-throwing – that is simply being self-indulgent and is not the same as suffering "because of me".)

Equally important is to recognise that we should never persecute others for their faith or lack of it, or for any reason at all. And sometimes persecution can be expressed in very subtle ways.

Learning hard lessons

There may be times when we need to learn something about ourselves. And for a reason beyond our understanding the particular lesson in question has to be taught to us through experiencing a tough situation. We are allowed to journey through some bad weather. (This is not saying that the bad weather is specifically, deliberately, caused for this purpose. The existence of suffering, great and small, is more complex.) Perhaps we lose friends, or the job stops going well. Perhaps some security in our life is taken away or we have to face disappointment in our past or in our future expectations. Such times are not easy. Yes, our perseverance and boat-craft are being strengthened, but it is still a painful season.

And sometimes the weather is just plain awful.

Of course we can equally learn about ourselves during the comfortable times. Whether it is a beautiful day or a storm-filled one, part of our calling is to become more self-aware, more able to be honest and open with ourselves. It is not always easy.

The pain of loss

Sometimes we will be sad. Something will have happened that causes us to weep. The reality of love means that we share in people's sufferings and we deeply grieve when we lose what is special to us (albeit temporarily – in terms of eternity we will never lose what has been truly good). Jesus himself wept at a funeral. A characteristic of Christian thinking is that it takes suffering seriously, realising that it hurts, that there are no slick responses and seldom an easy way through. The group does not glorify suffering, still less yearn for it, but honours and supports those who go through it. Grief can be a holy place; it speaks of love for the person and self. It is a place where Jesus himself stood.

It is not a sign of failure to be unhappy when things are sad. This sounds obvious, but there may be tempting voices saying that we always need to look happy. The world is not always a happy place. If it were, there would have been no need for Jesus or the ongoing work of the Spirit; we will sometimes see tears on the face of the captain as well as on our own.

The Bible verses about being joyful, Philippians 4:4 for example, are more to do with inner strength and assurance than having a perpetual smile on our face. Note Paul's clarification a few sentences later in verses 11-13 or the similarly magnificent 2 Corinthians 4:7-9.

Sickness, whether emotional, mental or physical, is part of the world we inhabit. Occasionally miracles happen and there are wonderful healings, direct divine foreshadowing of that time when, we are told, all suffering will cease. But, in biblical accounts and now, these are the exceptions. Until all things are renewed and there is indeed a "new heaven and a new earth", there will be suffering. All possible help and support are to be offered and sought. But the suffering still hurts.

And sometimes the weather is just plain awful.

Why do we have to put up with suffering at all?

This is an important question and a deeper answer would (and does) take up many books. In this short space all that can be done is to mention some points that may be helpful in thinking this through further.

A great deal of suffering is caused by our ability to hurt rather than help. Free will is sometimes a terrifying gift to possess. If we choose to destroy rather than build then that is our responsibility. We cannot blame anyone else.

But we will also note that a great deal of suffering is caused by the way our physical world works. A single death from cancer raises the same philosophical point as an earthquake destroying a city: death, tragically, is inexorably part of our present existence.

And there are the random deaths and injuries. A loss of concentration leading to a car accident, a tile falling from the roof at the wrong time. Not caused by evil or by natural forces; just happening, pointlessly, randomly.

Paul claims in Romans chapter 8, following many Old Testament prophecies, that the saving work of Jesus is one day going to encompass the whole physical world as well as humanity. He argues that the natural world itself is yearning for that final saving. It, like us, needs a new beginning. The offer and long-term plan for humanity is an existence in which there is no death or suffering.

That's all very well, but why do we have to wait? A much-visited theme in the Bible can be summarised by the question: "Why doesn't God put an end to all the suffering now?" In asking for an end to suffering we are asking for the end of the world as we know it. The world and humanity, with all the imperfections and suffering, are being allowed to run on a little longer. We may long for a speedier ending – this longing is echoed in the very last verses of the Bible – but if there is a God, then his sense of timing will be better than ours. We have to wait a little longer.

It hurts so much. Yes, suffering can be used to grow good qualities such as courage and love, but usually we would rather not have the suffering in the first place. The Christian belief is that God cares even more about it than we do; that is why Jesus came. He knows what it is to suffer and to weep. He knows the pain of crucifixion. The resurrection shows that death does not have the

And sometimes the weather is just plain awful.

last word. One day the tears will be wiped away.

But not yet, and that is sometimes very, very hard to bear.

As it is, of course, for all worldviews. Suffering does not go away despite a multitude of ideas, philosophies and religions. Christianity has the strength of seeing it as part of its narrative: suffering is caused by the nature of the world we live in and human fallen-ness (and there are some suggestions in the Bible that, beyond our understanding, the two may be linked). God knows what it is to suffer and one day suffering will cease because of Christ's saving work.

There is a constant wrestling in the Bible with this problem, and the answer tends to be along these lines: "I don't know why it has to be this way, but I still believe in God even though there are things I do not understand. My role is to prevent or alleviate it when I can, comfort those afflicted when I am able, to long for the day when it will cease, and to honour the patience, compassion and maturity that it can bring – this applies to my own suffering as well as that of others."

There are some who think that the fact that suffering is a problem is evidence that there might be a God. More in the next chapter.

We need to be well resourced (welcomed, nourished, praying, loved and loving) because there are no promises that this is an easy ride. There will be rocks and mists, blisters and sunburn. The journey may be unclear or suddenly grow very dark. It may seem a strange and lonely course for a while with no other boats in sight. We join this boat because we think it is the right one, not because we think it will necessarily provide the easiest route. The companionship may sometimes feel like 'home' but there will be times when the weather is bad or we do not understand what is happening, or both.

A very common assurance in the Bible is "Do not be afraid". Fear seems to be such a part of human existence that we frequently need to be reminded that we have been invited to be in the right group and that we will indeed be seen safely home. Often it is the uncertainty as to how we will handle events that scares us, as much as the events themselves. With the captain, we will make it through; perhaps battered and confused, but we will win.

And sometimes the weather is just plain awful.

To consider

- Are there times when it is difficult for you to stand up for justice in your situation?
- Do you know of occasions when Christians are persecuted?
- If we are asking for all suffering to stop today, what are we asking for?
- How do we feel about being asked to believe in a God when we do not understand everything about his timing or the way he works?
- Occasionally the view is expressed: "get on board and all your problems will disappear" – how would you respond to that?

Chapter 15

Is the boat really there?

There are some who feel this chapter is unnecessary. They have never doubted that there is a God. But others may feel that, while some of the time we believe that there is Something (or perhaps even Someone) there, we have other moments when we wonder if the whole thing is simply made up.

We may even have heard people say or imply that faith is a brainless exercise and that those who believe there is anything out there are sad and deluded. They are just a bunch of individuals united by strange ideas and there is no captain at the heart of it. Is the boat really there? Are we being tempted by a glossy sales pitch, but in reality the company went bankrupt years ago and never had a genuine product to offer? In a nutshell, is it true?

Our important life choices very seldom rely on physical evidence. We enter a career, friendship or marriage because of numerous intangible pointers; we know that a complete set of concrete proofs is unlikely to be available. A sign that reportedly hung in Albert Einstein's office reminded visitors that "Not everything that counts can be counted, and not everything that can be counted counts." Rather a lot of our major life decisions involve faith – we have a certain amount of evidence but there is always an element of the unprovable and uncertain ("The new job looks good but I cannot guarantee that the boss won't change"). So we have to make the jump.

So what are the pointers for Christianity? Why might this be the right group? Why do so many people think that there is enough evidence for the jump to be worth making?

We may think that it would be so much easier if we could see or touch God, but in reality it would cause more difficulties. If God were visible and tangible he would be within and part of our physical universe. If God is God, then he needs to be bigger than that.

(And of course the Christian narrative says that God did appear on earth in Jesus; at one point in history he was touchable and the reactions were exactly the mix of adoration, rejection, fear and uncertainty that we would expect.)

The full list of evidence that has proved useful to people runs into many volumes, and different factors will have different weight for different people. Here are eight pointers that sometimes help. They are not 'knock down' arguments – the big decisions in life tend not to work like that – but they have been enough to make me feel that a faith position is a sensible and reasonable one to hold.

1. *The vast majority of humanity throughout history has believed in some sort of God.* The atheist argues that they all are completely wrong. The agnostic, more humbly, feels there is not enough evidence to agree or disagree with these multitudes. The Christian can see truths in many faiths and respect them, honouring our agreements and disagreements, uniting with them in affirming belief in the divine while still maintaining the belief that truth is most fully found in Christianity. Let us here simply note that there is a spiritual hunger across all cultures and backgrounds. Any other hunger is the response to

the existence of the object desired. Physical hunger is met in bread, emotional hunger in relationships. The desire to worship implies that somewhere there may be some sort of God.

2. *We are all shaped by those whom we meet.* I keep coming across people with gentle, persistent faith, still strong and growing whatever they have been through. Observing their lifestyle and courage I can't help but think that there is some sort of reality behind their belief. Thinking wider, I note also the presence of faith in the lives of so many significant thinkers and campaigners in history. At the very least, we need to take this seriously. Can such a variety of people – from Alfred the Great to Elizabeth I to Martin Luther King to Mother Teresa to Elvis Presley to J.R.R. Tolkien to child X next door and widow Y down the road – all be *completely* wrong? If I am hesitant to say that they are utterly deluded, then I need to ask how I can find out more about this common factor that they seem to share.

3. *The historicity of Jesus.* Jesus of Nazareth is unique in world history in what, according to the records, he said and did. There are ref-

erences in Jewish and Roman literature to Jesus as well as the historical records in the New Testament. The validity of the biblical record is a crucial issue. These records have rightly been challenged, tested and analysed more than any other documents in history but still they hold up.

As always in serious questioning, the key requirement is open-mindedness. If we study Jesus while refusing in any circumstances to accept the existence of the divine then that says more about our initial faith position than it does about our historical open-mindedness. If we study Jesus, willing to see where the evidence leads, then it is hard to avoid the conclusion that something extraordinary was happening.

Trying to leave all faith presuppositions behind, for and against, it is clear that something deeply significant happened around 30AD in that particular corner of the Roman Empire. All the old dreams and glimpses of a life bigger than the physical were claimed to have been fulfilled in a tangible person in our human story. It was an intellectual and materialistic period in European history. People would have needed very good reasons to believe something so outlandish as the claims surrounding this carpenter's son from Galilee. They seemed to have found those good reasons.

4. *The problem of suffering.* Whether or not we believe in God, suffering exists. We see children suffer in a far-off country and we not only say: "That is so sad" or "I'm glad that is not happening to me," we also say: "This should not be happening, they don't deserve this". The use of words such as "should" and "deserve" imply a sense of moral framework where compassion and justice are highly prized. It speaks of a sense, a deep memory, that the world should not be like this; this matches the Christian narrative that humanity is in some way fallen and our world is flawed. The fact that we respond so strongly to suffering happening far away from us does not sit easily with the idea that we are simply a collection of chemicals. We may ask: "If there is a God of love, why is there so much suffering?" An equally significant question is, "If there is *not* a God of love, why does suffering matter so much?"

5. *We react powerfully to beauty and to new life.* Consider the joy and wonder of seeing a new-

born baby. Consider our reaction to sunsets, art, sport or music. When we sense the vastness of the universe we use words such as 'awesome'. Where do these feelings, this appreciation, come from? Perhaps our response to creativity, beauty and new life is an echo of the nature of a creative God.

6. *Intuitions.* There seem to be times when some people experience something they can only describe as including some sense of the 'other', of the spiritual, perhaps of God. I could try to explain these moments away but then feel that I am not being true to what people tell me, and indeed to my own small experiences.

7. *We live in a universe of amazing order, variety and complexity.* Another Einstein quotation: "One may say the eternal mystery of the world is its comprehensibility." Why should it follow any pattern at all? Why should we be able to understand so much of it? We are accustomed to think in terms of laws of nature. It is possible that the presence of such laws is a pointer to the existence of a creative and ordered mind.

8. *We desire meaning and purpose.* We want to know that we matter. If we hear

Shakespeare's Macbeth declaim that life "is a tale told by an idiot, full of sound and fury, signifying nothing", we feel that is not a healthy view to take. Perhaps it could be argued that it is only wishful thinking to hope for a value beyond being a collection of molecules. But it is significant that this wishful thinking itself exists. We want to be more than eating and breeding machines. The very fact that we ask existential questions may mean that existence is bigger than the tangible.

* * *

These eight pointers, and more could be added, are not here to convince. They are simply here to remind us that it is perfectly reasonable for people to think that there is a God. It is a step of faith, like all big decisions, but it is a step based on a considerable amount of evidence.

To consider

- These 'pointers for belief' listed above – which help you and which do not?
- Are there others that you would add?

- Do you have specific questions you would like to ask about evidence for God? If so, whom will you ask or what might you read?
- "There are some who feel this chapter is unnecessary." They feel their own experience is strong and certain enough. How do you respond to them?

Chapter 16

Or picnics, buses and dancing?

It is a risk using an image as a theme for a book. Perhaps some readers get violently sea-sick and the whole idea of getting on a boat is off-putting. We will have different images in our mind when we read the word 'boats', and likewise 'harbour' (I realise I have had a particular harbour in mind throughout this book; your mental picture of a harbour may be completely different). And there are limits to the analogy: if we get on the Christian boat, then does that mean we are not constantly mingling with others? Surely that is not following in the footsteps of Jesus, who spent rather a lot of time doing such mingling.

So at one point the image was changed to 'taking a walk'. The harbour side became a picnic area at a view point and two characters had to choose which walking group they would choose for the next stage of the journey. The point was made that everyone is in some sort of group. (Even those who saw themselves as 'rugged individualists' were in a group of like-minded people, but walked apart from each other and did not talk to each other very much.) These groups are continually bumping into each other as they make their way down the mountain. Jesus became the leader of a group rather than the captain of a boat.

Would a bus station work? Getting on the right bus in the middle of a grey and damp town does not sound as attractive. But then harbours can be unappealing in some weathers and should the picture be attractive in any case? Perhaps some grittiness is more helpful than a postcard scene.

Or a barn dance? Everyone having steps to take, not only for their own sake but also for the sake of the wider dance and all those in it. The necessity of listening to the one who is calling the steps. Unity and diversity, structure and freedom, open to all.

The imagery and parallels should not be taken too far. But it is helpful to remember that our choice of image can affect the way we see things and indeed the way we live our lives. Two friends, only half-jokingly, used to see how much they could compare life situations to a chess game. Others use characters: Some may identify with Frodo Baggins, battling against all odds to fulfil a quest. Others may see themselves more as Alice, learning to cope with a Wonderland where nothing makes sense and everything has the possibility to be slightly scary. And, of course, these identifications may not be happening on the conscious level.

An important connected issue is the image that we have of God. Some have an image of God as someone remote or frightening, for others it is the opposite: a Father Christmas figure who ultimately does not mind much what we do. Neither of these are Christian images and it is always helpful to ponder where these false images come from. In Christian belief the most accurate and authoritative image of God is Jesus. In John, chapter 14, Jesus says: "Anyone who has seen me has seen the Father." In his letter to the Colossians, chapter 1, Paul describes Jesus as "the image of the invisible God". For those of us exploring Christianity, Jesus is the image of God that is offered to us.

And that means that we will need to turn to our Bibles and read those accounts of his life.

Captain of the boat, Leader of the walking group, Bus driver (and ticket collector who has bought our tickets with his own money?), Caller at the Barn Dance? As we draw to a close we may as well keep with the harbour side image but, as stated at the beginning, it is the content, not the wrapping, which matters.

To consider

- Do images help you to consider the big questions of life and faith or are they a distraction?

- "Our choice of image can affect the way we see things and indeed the way we live our lives." Do you agree?

- What is your image of God? Where does it come from?

Chapter 17

What next?

The boats are still there, bobbing in the waves in the quietness of the inner harbour. Beyond the breakwater the sea is rougher and the conditions more uncertain. You know that the boats are all slightly different, all promising slightly different journeys and destinations. They may look different, too: small and large, battered and glossy; but you know that the appearance is less important than the underlying seaworthiness of the craft. Is this boat going to get there? Is it well-captained?

There are different boats. One may contain crew members who seek to gain as much money as possible, seeing it as a means to an end, believing it can bring freedom from worry, or status, or friends or the envy of others. But if you are interested in forgiveness, eternal life, love for others as they are and yourself as you are, then this crew will not deliver, and does not promise to do so.

One boat may promise salvation through becoming as perfect as you can. You will be accepted into heaven by keeping all the rules. It is held together by the glue of perfectionism and fear rather than love and grace. We will always have the nagging sense that this is an impossible task.

Another boat makes no promise at all for a destination. Here the captain does not believe there is a heaven, God, ultimate meaning or value.

And so on: a myriad of boats below you, bobbing in the harbour. We all choose some sort of boat, some structure of reference points, some sort of captain to trust.

What is on offer in the Christian boat? Jesus promised this: "I have come that they may have life, and have it to the full." Caught up in this is the promise of a deep, fulfilled life that will last beyond death; of rich and growing relationships with others and with God; we becoming the people we were always meant to be. It is a profound and enormous promise: Restoration, Growth, Heaven.

Most people in the world think there is some sort of God, however differently they express this belief. Many groups do all they can to help people get close to this God, insisting on various disciplines and rituals. Christianity sees it the other way round. God has come to rescue us, to pick us up as we are, to welcome us home. When he sees us begin to approach the gangplank he rushes down it to greet us. God does not meet us halfway; he meets us all the way. That is what the whole Jesus story is about.

But it is an invitation, not a forced march onto a slave boat. It is about love, not compulsion. We can refuse.

It will have been a full and important journey to reach this harbour side. Already we have experienced joys and sorrows, times of growth and times of frustrations; we have met a rich variety of people. There have been times when we have been treated well, times when we have been treated badly. That's the way it is. But we know the journey carries on.

The pause has been valuable. The sea spreads out in front of us. In our imagination our sight grows wider and we see more broadly. Over there the sun is glinting on a quiet sea; further on the waves are towering and the storm is raging.

To the right the fog has fallen and all seems flat and gloomy. Various islands are dotted across the ocean. You see many different boats on different courses. Sometimes they cross each other's paths. Some seem to have gone a certain distance but then stopped, either on one of the islands or simply still in the water. Then, as if our eyes are strengthened further, we see a course set through the islands, through the different weathers, through the varied currents, to a land to the east in the far distance, as if to the edge of the world.

It will be quite something being in the boat that follows the course towards the rising sun.

What next?

You may feel you want to explore Christianity further. Find a Christian and ask what it is like for them. Discuss with friends where you feel the thinking in this book is helpful and where it is weak or frustrating, or discuss what it was that brought you to consider such things in the first place. Many churches run groups for those who want know more.

You may feel that you have heard enough, here and elsewhere, and believe that this is the boat you want to join. You may feel that here is a captain worth finding out more about, a leader worth trusting, a leader worth following. If so, take the step of saying a quiet "yes" to Jesus, however tentative or firm. Perhaps look back again at chapters 3 and 5. Find a local group of fellow travellers (there will be more around than you think) and continue the journey of prayer, learning, sacraments and community. It may be an encouragement to know that millions and millions have stood where you are standing, have felt that this boat is right for them, and would say that the journey onwards has been good. Not always easy, comfortable or straightforward, but ultimately, deeply, satisfyingly, good.

You may of course already be part of the Christian boat and simply wished to read someone else's thoughts. Perhaps you could consider what you would have said if you had been writing a book like this. All our emphases and insights will be slightly different; that is part of the fun of the voyage.

Wherever you are on the journey, thank you for taking the time to read this. I wish you well.

Anthony Buckley

Appendix

Chapter 6 continued... Suggested readings from the Bible

If you want a selection of shorter passages that cover a variety of themes, you may wish to use this list of passages, enough for a month.

Three Bible writers' sense of purpose

1. 2 Timothy 3:16
    (*2 Timothy* is the name of the book; *3* is the chapter number; *16* is the verse number)
2. Luke 1:1-4
3. John 20:31

Two Old Testament writers' perception of God and faith

4. Psalm 23:1-6
5. Habakkuk 3:17,18

Events and teachings from the life of Jesus

6. Luke 15:11-32
7. Luke 5:17-26
8. Matthew 5:1-49
9. Matthew 6:1-34
10. Matthew 7:1-29
11. Mark 4:35-41
12. John 3:16
13. John 10:10
14. Mark 10:13-16
15. Matthew 28:16-20
16. John 6:35
17. John 6:68
18. John 8:57-59
19. John 1:1-14
20. Matthew 11:28-30

The early church begins to work out what being followers of Jesus means

21. Acts 2:42-47
22. 1 Corinthians 12:12-22
23. 1 Corinthians 13:1-13
24. 1 Corinthians 15:1-14
25. 1 Peter 2:23-25
26. Romans 8:1-17
27. Romans 8:18-39
28. Philippians 4:1-13

29. 1 John 1:8,9
30. Galatians 5:22-26

Someday, things will change

31. Revelation 21:1-5

The list is designed simply as an introduction. Do move on from these to other readings.